Sanctuary

PATRICIA MONAGHAN

salmonpoetry

Published in 2013 by
Salmon Poetry
Cliffs of Moher, County Clare, Ireland
Website: www.salmonpoetry.com
Email: info@salmonpoetry.com

ISBN 978-1-908836-51-9

COVER PHOTOGRAPHY: *Jessie Lendennie*
COVER DESIGN & TYPESETTING: *Siobhán Hutson*

Printed in Ireland by Sprint Print

Salmon Poetry gratefully acknowledges the support of The Arts Council

Contents

PART TWO: *Land Mass*

Introduction

Patricia Monaghan passed away at Brigit Rest, her beloved land in Black Earth, Wisconsin on November 11, 2012. She was comforted and attended by me, her husband. This collection takes the reader to experiences, dreams, lessons and hopes of a poet valuing place in a world too often where as she wrote 'place is a verb.'

Sanctuary is a tale rooted in two places, Ireland, mostly the West, and the Driftless Area of Wisconsin in the United States. These two places were precious to Patricia as locales to appreciate their present and past. They are linked as places lived in, by geography and as places of history that cry out for discovery of the sacredness of the land and settings for guidance in how to live with value and connection. Some of these poems were pictures of geology, some of the living earth's evolution, some reminders of those peoples, creatures and spirits that came before and those who are right in front of us if we know how to look. Some are even outright recipes for how to live.

The West of Ireland, the location of most the work of 'Book of Hours' has been filled with wildness and yet preservation of time and beliefs. The West has inspired poets, playwrights, and folklorists from medieval and modern times. Yeats, Synge, Lady Gregory among others found in the West a way to bring basic human truths to an Ireland desperate for its own values and identity. Patricia found it so for finding her own connections to her past but more for bringing these pictures to all who would see.

She and I had been in the places so skillfully recreated in 'Book' and each one roars out its detailed particularity in which we were immersed at the time. We reveled in the richness of beauty, beauty and discovery when there and she was delighted to recreate and even deepen those revelations for others to share and see.

The West of Ireland remains wild and attracts pilgrims even after the mushrooming of holiday homes, now vacant, from the now familiar housing financing boom and bust common to the two countries.

Patricia first spent time near the area studying Yeats in Gort near Coole Woods, Lady Gregory's estate and Thoor Ballylee celebrated in his poems. From there she found Connemara and its mountains and bogs. *The Red-Haired Girl from the Bog*, her book on the spiritual geography of Ireland came from these findings.

A special place outside the West was Kildare, the home of St. Brigit and now the locale of the Brigit revival and ceremony each spring. The holy well of St. Brigit and before that of the Celtic goddess were a place for uniting the past and present. Brigit's Eve, January 31, 2013, a wonderful celebration of Celtic spirituality, remembered Patricia in a special mention by her step-daughter Emily.

The Driftless Area or as it is also called the Paleozoic Plateau is unique in North America and is the setting for 'Land Mass'. Consisting of 16,300 square miles mainly in South Central Wisconsin the area was not glaciated during at least the Wisconsin glacier. The topography is one of ridges of deep valleys without the flatness or myriad lakes characteristic of much of the American upper Midwest. Much of the area is called 'coulee country', drawn from the French for 'deep valley' and from the hundred plus years of French dominance of early European penetration into the region. The varied terrain and biodiversity of the area served as a rich source of sustenance for the Native peoples who had lived there before. Only after the Black Hawk war and the mass slaughter of 1837 did large scale European settlement take place. Some of the attraction was the lead and silver mining nearby centered in what is now called Blue Mounds. This drew Cornish miners and Irish labor to the area. The signs of these European peoples can still found in village and road names as well as Cornish festivals in old mining towns. Brigit

Rest, Patricia's home in Wisconsin, is in sight of these Blue Mounds across nine miles of ridges. She gardened, maintained a vineyard, cleared brush and loved the area. There is an immediate sense of weather and seasons with specific tasks and observations for each time.

The detailed view of geology, topography, plants, animals, spirits and human behavior throughout celebrate the close observation and appreciation surrounding us, often ignored in modern life. The pictures immerse one in these details in a way that makes such ignoring impossible and uncomfortable. The connections between Ireland and the Driftless Area are also demanded by the history of the peoples.

We found a cemetery naming local Irish families as coming from Ballyvourney, County Cork. Once in Ballyvourney we found St. Gobnait's well and wondered at the loss of such connection for a figure well known throughout Cork and beyond and yet forgotten by Wisconsin Irish Americans. Like so many Irish immigrants in America it was often too painful and "foreign" to keep these connections alive and yet they exist to be portrayed.

Patricia grew up in Alaska and never quite adjusted to the huge city of Chicago where she worked, lived and taught for many years. The qualities of Ireland and the Driftless Area gave her comfort and the opportunity for challenge, discovering and deeper meaning. I often felt the same. I was and am privileged for her life, work and spirit. She not only created visions of a better world but built structures to bring these visions to reality. These continue in Brigit Rest, the Black Earth Insitute and the Association for the Study of Women and Mythology as well as her work and friends she influenced.

We will miss her but these poems will help her live on.

MICHAEL MCDERMOTT
February 11, 2013

Book of Hours

INVITATORY: LAUDS

That boreen that circles the big turlough,
its bramble hedges reckless with growth:

I want to walk there in the pale dawn
in spring, deep in the shadow of the hill,

to hear the soft sound of countless birds
awakening from downy sleep and of rivulets

bubbling toward the sea and of small dark-furred
hunters on their secret paths. No wind disturbs

the grass; all is still; deep dust muffles even
my footsteps; time halts; stars dim into pearl.

I want to be walking forever, always on the way
towards a kitchen garden planted with sweet peas

and marrows, with herbs and plums and roses,
I want to be forever almost there, about to arrive,

not quite at the cottage door, I want the scent
of fresh bread to offer me its yeasty promises,

I want never to arrive, never to break out of darkness
into the yellow half-circle of light from the kitchen door,

always to have one foot lifted into the next step,
always to have one arm lifted in greeting.

THINGS WORTH PRAISING

Rain. Soft rain. Hard pelting rain. Sleet and snow.
Clouds: white, grey, dark. A spring breeze.
The predictability of stars and moon and sun.

Green small hills. Craggy slopes. Granite cliffs.
Topsoil deep and rich. The melody of rivers.
The power of tides. The cycle of change.

Industry of bee and worm. Sweet fruit that follows.
Microbes that make cheese. Ones that cure us.
Profound cooperation that begets lichen.

Birdsong carried on wind. The shadow of a horse
against a limestone wall. A dog's warmth.
Blood. Flesh. Bones. Hearts. Breath.

A friend's hand, reaching out for help or tea.
A sigh, a song, an honest smile, a body dancing.
Everything that connects and is connected. Everything.

MORNING, THOOR BALLYLEE

The millwheel is still, its river
gone carousing through the meadow.

In a deep crack in the wheel's face,
grass and lichen find a haven.

A thin green line snakes across
the granite disc. Light stipples

the silent millhouse, its slate
roof fallen to the stone floor.

Stinging nettles guard the door.
The sun shines, the millstone

shines, the stone walls shine.
A bee hangs in the holy air.

SAINT GOBNAIT'S DEER

An angel told that sharp-featured
woman, Mo Gobnait, to find

nine white deer grazing together.
"That is your place of resurrection,"

the angel said. Gobnait set forth
and soon found three deer, grazing

peaceably in Clondrohid. Gobnait
kept walking until she saw six deer

grazing together in Ballymakeera.
She kept walking. And the deer

walked too, the three and the six
coming together at last to graze

at Ballyvourney, right beside
the river Sullane. There Gobnait

stopped. Did she feel the air
grow thin with presence? Did

she sing her homecoming song?
Did she fall to her knees and pray?

What would you do, if you knew
you stood in the place of your death?

SEEKING THE WELL

The Ordinance Survey map was clear:
west of a castle ruin, beyond a three-way
cross, beside a spring-fed lake, we'd find
a holy well. A red dot showed just where.

I could almost see the gnarled beribboned
tree reflected, like the slate-blue sky, in
a small pool of clear bubbling water, its
soft banks printed by fallow deer and hare.

I saw how the sky would lighten as we neared
and the soft-eyed deer would lift her head
from the well and stare at us as the hare
bounded away and the wind shook the tree,

for is this not the way spirit moves on earth?
Everything clear and beautiful. Everything
beautiful and clear. Well water, sky water,
liquid animal eyes, sea-skeletons in limestone.

The map was clear. There could be no mistake.
We reached the site and found a ruined wall.
A dog ran through a ragged gap, yellow, panting.
A horse whinnied on the hill behind us.

Behind the wall, a meager reedy field
and one white cow. No deer, no hare,
no clootie tree, no well. Just field and cow,
and a strong salt wind from the slate-blue sea.

A GARDEN NEAR THE SEA

Two low stone walls: shelter enough to start a garden
where burdock and ragwort and nettles massed together.

I begin to dig a long straight bed, surprised to find purple
mint, dwarf rose and lily-of-the-valley, a struggling willow,

spikes of montbrezia, escaped geranium. And slate and granite
enough to build a curving wall to protect a tiny hidden spring.

Ten thousand years ago, melting glaciers left those rocks,
gifts to the land. Ten thousand years from now, the sea

may cover this field again. Change will come sooner too:
some plants will die in salty wind, nettles will invade again,

my little wall will collapse in rain. A garden is beauty's
temporary home, but gardening is hope in action. So I dig.

LESSONS FROM TREES

Cottonwood in early summer:
    Hollowness, extravagance, luxury.
Oak, near a bedrock well:
    The evidence of sorrow. A failure to dance.
Willow, twisted into diamonds:
    A single cruel act suffices.

Dying spruce among cedar:
    Grandeur, singularity, doom.
Blasted sycamore beside a stream:
    A chasm in the heart. Leave at once.
Graven oak in a walled garden:
    Preserve the dark hollows of memory.

Cherry, burdened with sweetness:
    Longing, loneliness, abandon.
Birch, split in four sections:
    Hope's cruel beauty. The path divides.
Yew, on a cliff near the sea:
    Someone danced here once, alone.

SAINT GOBNAIT'S BEES

"Irish bees untroubled by colony collapse"
Irish Times, Thursday, May 5, 2011

Settled down in Ballyvourney,
Gobnait took to raising bees.

She had a knack for it. Her bees
were happy in their wicker hives,

and Gobnait had honey enough
to make the healing remedies

for which she was renowned.
Her bees loved her so much

that when Ballyvourney came
under attack, the bees flew forth

and drove the foe away. Did
their stings serve as weapons

or did they, as some say, turn
into tiny soldiers to wage war?

Is there any difference? Gobnait
rested safely in her beehive hut

as the fight raged on. Afterwards
the bees returned to their flowery work

and Gobnait to her healing. When
she died, bees sang in remembrance.

BOOK OF HOURS

Monks read the "office" for each hour,
the name derived from Latin *ops*,
 "power," and related to *opus*, "work."

> *(Let us pray: for a time when power*
> *remembers its relationship to work.)*

But lay folk read a shorter version,
called "books of hours," celebrating
dawn and dusk and midnight.

> *(Let us pray: for a time when time's*
> *passage again gives cause for celebration.)*

Such "books" were not, as the word
suggests, written on leaves of "beech,"
but on vellum or parchment or paper.

> *(Let us pray: for a time when we recall*
> *the basis of wisdom in the earth.)*

And the "hours" were once "seasons"
before the meaning changed to artificial
measurements of passing time.

> *(Let us pray: for a time when nature,*
> *not clocks, measures out our lives.)*

What is today's holy office? Where
is our book of hours? How can we claim
again the spirit's dignity? How can we not?

EVENSONG

Southwest off the coast, dusky pink
and lavender paint the clouds.

To the north, a lowering sky
like watery ink on gray paper.

A thin moon sits on the horizon
above the sea, beside a single star.

As night gathers like clouds,
we wrap ourselves in twilight

as in a garment of rain. Then,
hooded in our somber cloaks,

we pray that light remembers us
as we traverse the darkness.

LATIARAN'S HEART

Three holy women came westward
from France to that place on the border

of Kerry and Cork where the great paps
rise, Danu's giant mist-clad breasts:

Lasair, the eldest, stopped at Killasseragh
and made a hermit's cell her home;

and the middle sister, the yellow-haired one,
went along the Blackwater to Dromtarriff

and stopped her journey there; and
the youngest, Latiaran, went to coal-rich

Cullen, where a smith gave her embers
every day to heat her hut. She carried

the embers back in her apron and spent
her days in prayer and contemplation.

Then one day the smith complimented
her shapely feet and Latiaran's apron

burst into flame and she uttered a curse
that no smith would ever thrive in Cullen

and she disappeared, leaving behind
only a granite stone beside the road.

Her curse still holds. No blacksmith lives
in Cullen now to give away embers

and compliment the women. What's
left of Latiaran? A heart-shaped stone.

STONE HOUSE IN HIGH WIND

1

Sun shines through slanted rain.
On the strand, limpets crack
under the weight of waves,
and we imagine men at sea
clinging to shuddering masts.

2

Sword-branched trees batter
darkening windows as
the storm advances
on helpless hills.

3

A dancing black star
befriends the wind.
A woman in scarlet
carries a brass horn
across a forest hill.

4

Light the candle, friend,
and tell me what you most dread.

5

Wind as wolf.
Wind as demon's breath.
Wind as cavern of yearning.

CONNEMARA AUTUMN

A few more weeks and winter's hand will run
across the bramble fruit and poison it.
But no one picks what glistens in the sun
along the roadsides. Small birds hide within

the hedgerow thorns and fatten on the fruit.
The hedges seed and spread, engulfing
old stone walls and wooden fences. Minute
by minute, mystery removes itself from us.

The men who married women of the sea
have moved inland and taken human wives.
Dogs run wild among the sheep, which flee
into the granite hills. Even the crows fall silent.

PSALM OF THE SPARROW

What is the difference
between blood and a song?

When does the moon start
to be a round eye?

What does it matter
what anything means?

Why not let blood
sing blue in your veins?

HOW TO CONFESS

Distinguish from: regret.
Distinguish from: remorse.
Distinguish from: shame.

Look for: excuses.
Look for: denial.
Look for: blame.

Examine: how you speak.
Examine: how you act.
Examine: where you aim.

Think of: who you hurt.
Think of: what you harmed.
Think: what you inflamed.

Find: the ear of god.
Find: a hollow shell.
Find: if they're the same.

Speak: what did you do?
Speak: what was the harm?
Speak. Acknowledge. Claim.

LATIARAN'S WELL

Not long before she stamped her foot
and disappeared, leaving behind

only her rough stone heart,
Latiaran planted a whitethorn tree—

the tree of satirists, the tree sacred
to ancient goddesses of spring—

beside the Owentaraglen
which flows into the Blackwater.

As she disappeared, a spring welled
up beneath the tree, and to it came

the blind, the halt, the sick, the lame;
the impoverished, bereft and mad.

They drank the water. Some were cured,
some comforted, and some unchanged,

and there was no way to tell which would
be which: good people left, still blind, while

cheats and braggarts threw away their canes,
and sometimes it was the other way around.

We do not earn our grace or griefs, our pain
or our relief from pain. It's all a mystery.

The thorn tree blooms. The water flows.
Latiaran disappeared and never went away.

ON THE FAMINE ROAD

"How can men feel themselves honoured by the humiliation of their fellow human beings?"

MAHATMA GANDHI

How did it begin?
    In the big house, men
    dined with other men.

And was the weather bad?
    The crop, healthy at first,
    rotted as though cursed.

Was there no other food?
    Cattle-filled ships, every day,
    set sail to take the meat away.

Who was lost?
    The dogs grew fat. Mothers tried
    to fend them off as children died.

Did no one object?
    Those without food, given bread,
    refuse to work, they said.

What is this path?
    Even the grass is hungry here.
    Hundreds died, with food so near.

GRACE AT TABLE

Here is a woman who prayed for healing and fell ill.
Here is a man who lives in faith, without hope.
Here is a woman who has lost her girlhood.
Here is a man who was never fully a boy.

We break bread together and eat the season:

Here is lamb, killed early in the mountain fall.
Here is fish, pulled yesterday from its ocean home.
Here are carrots, torn last week from the stony soil.
Here, apples from autumn's heavy harvest.

Death sits at our table. We are filled with unspeakable joy.

KEEPING VIGIL IN RENVYLE

We pass the hours measuring the weather:
the Twelve Bens emerge and then dissolve
in mist and pearly cloud; a dim storm gathers
over Tully Mountain, breaks above us, then resolves

itself in light mist on the Diamond's crest.
We watch the moon illuminate the lake
which dulls then to a sheen of gray. Just west
the sea, invisible from here, makes

all this happen. All night the waiting wind
tests every wall. Within, we dream
of animals reincarnating as our kin,
of spirits rising from the bogs like steam.

KILLARY HARBOUR

Blue boats pass beneath watercolor peaks
through pale water, colored slate
with silt. Suspended between dawn and day
a relict pier peers down at glittery lattices.
The boats have long obtained the bay mouth
when the first slap against the shelly shore
pulls down the tinseled mask of stasis from
the face of loss. The relict groans, attenuated
with anticipation, and then, then, then, the slap,
slap, slap, all the spent largesse of memory
expended in blue deposits of stone and coin,
washed glass and skeletons and sand,
raided from the deep and other shores,
like sorrows surging up in vivid dreams.

BRIGIT MOURNS HER
SON RUADAN

Down paths of ash and alder, down a corridor
of yew, she walked and walked, blind with sorrow.

Day after day she walked the forest, sometimes weeping,
sometimes stunned with pain and wordless grieving.

More than one death: so many, so much pain, so much despair.
The paths led nowhere. The trees were stark and bare.

But then one day all was different. Where before
the way was dark and straight, now the forest floor

was a maze of freedoms she had never seen.
She lost her bearings, wandered aimless, in a dream

of dappled leaf, of greening light. In this new world
she came upon an oak tree, huge and old and burled.

It was alive. She saw this, knew this, suddenly.
Of course, the whole forest was alive, each tree

lived just as fully as that oak. But in her pain
she had stopped seeing how all around her, life sustained

itself, right unto death. That tree, in vast and rooted
strength, stood there so vividly alive that it refuted

any silent argument with life, life which blazed
from every leaf and branch like psalms of praise.

And that tree saw her. Heard her. Knew her, she knew it did.
For just a moment, that tree was all the god she needed.

The light did not fade or die. No, it was she who turned
back to the path, she who walked away, an imprint burned

upon her soul by what she'd seen. In sleep she stares
into the eyes of ancient oaks, regal, strong, aware.

EPISTLES FROM DEAD FRIENDS

Two letters in familiar hands: two
dead friends who never knew each other
appear from different sources, impromptu,
unexpected. "I am unhappier
than you might think," says one,
and the other, "I hope that you are wrapped
around with love." Both met oblivion
through cancer, but each friend mapped
the route to death so differently, Ed
angry all the way, Barbara radiant
with hope. What matter? Both are dead,
gone beyond both joy and discontent.
But Barbara wrote of seeing double rainbows,
Ed of nursing grudges, right to the close.

WIND LITURGY

I saw nothing but bog and sky,
shallow lakes, scrub grass,
and the gray distant mountains.

And rock. Bones of the bog,
jutting from the thin flesh
of grass and shining water.

I stood on a granite ledge,
staring into the blue sky.
Clouds formed and reformed.

On the open bog, the wind
was fierce and cold. I stood
open and cold, in the wind.

After a time, the wind spoke.
It spoke the way the wind speaks.
Its words were whispered clarity.

And I spoke back to the wind.
And the wind answered.
And I spoke again to the wind.

The bog stirred, shaking its
grassy head, and the sky stirred,
tossing its cloudy head, and

I disappeared into the wind,
until it was I who
stirred the clouds and grass,

it was I who sang that wordless
song, it was I who pushed
against the gray mountains

and tore them slowly down,
and it was I who carried the bee
fertilizing the gorse and heather,

and even now, the wind possesses
me, and sings this song through me,
whistling fiercely in your ear.

BRIGIT INVENTS WHISTLING

Before she was abbess and saint,
when Brigit was still a goddess,
she invented two things.

We know the story of the first:
when Ruadan, her only son,
was killed, Brigit's soul ripped

open into sound, shredding
the air with grief, tearing tears
from all eyes: the first keening.

But whistling, now: legend
does not reveal why Brigit
first pursed her lips and blew.

Except for this: it was at night.
Can you picture it? The goddess
sitting on a flat gray rock

looking at the moonlit sea
and hearing small sounds
from the darkening earth:

moans, murmurs, rustles,
rumbles, chitters, creaks,
barks and buzzes, echoes,

and her blood roared
in her ears, her heart boomed,
and she became all music

and vibration, so that even
the stars and moon danced
to the unsounded sounds

of her breathing body,
and then it all rushed out of her:
a whistle in the night.

LESSONS FROM BIRDS

Gray sparrow, dead, in front of a door:
      Do not hold yourself aloof from what is coming.
      Suspense and fulfillment, complete emptiness.
      Embrace strange animals for the full answer.

Seagull at noon, crying louder than bells:
      Who comes now will be blessed and burdened.
      Serving and commanding: one and the same.
      Dreams will not matter, only omens.

Mourning doves, nesting above a door:
      Every thread is part of the inevitable design.
      Weeping and consoling, the same sound.
      It will fall. It is only a matter of when.

Falcon, like a guardian of the circle:
      Even simple things grow complicated at the end.
      A beak like a knife. An eye like a knife.
      Lie on a volcano's rim and look down.

Raven, on a chair, screaming:
      You have come home. Come home.
      Underfoot, fragrances and poisons.
      From blue distances, the sound of rain.

Owl, just before dawn, in the street:
      Who goes now was never really here.
      Light and shadow, a matter of position.
      What is the only direction a song can move?

EVE, AFTERWARDS

How can I tell you, in words, what it was like,
before words? Before names interposed themselves

between us and the world? Before life became
fragmented, hardened into atoms of meaning?

It was like this: I would see a flower, yellow
under a blue sky, and I would not think "flower,"

or "blue," or "yellow," or "sky," I would not think
"perfume" or "softness" or "springtime" or "fragility"—

my eyes would hear the evanescent color
of each petal's wavering line, my hand

would see how soft the yellow rested
in the bloom, I would drink the slow sound

of the roots, breathe sharp leaf greenness,
hear endless staccato motioning of bees.

When I say I was in love with Eden
I mean exactly that: every moment I caressed

its unnamed beauties with my eyes,
my hands, my mouth, my senses, held it

to me like a lover, memorized its shapes,
its brilliant shadows, its endless light, each

wordless eternal moment is alive in me
still, and when you ask me, where was Eden,

how can I show you it is here, hallowing
this moment, hallowing us in this moment—

oh look! that tree! oh look!

DAWN AT BRIGIT'S WELL

In hope, in pain, in song we passed the night.
We have kept watch—kept faith—each in our way.
Our long dark vigil ends in spring's mild light.

We ended winter with this ancient rite,
Strangers until we joined our hands to pray.
In hope, in pain, in song we passed the night.

Beside the guttering candles, a single white
Snowdrop nods to greet St. Brigit's day.
A long dark vigil ends in spring's mild light.

So much is wrong, across the world: we fight
Each other, blight the land, betray
Our hopes. In plaintive song we passed the night.

Yet we believe and pray, acolytes
In service to a change too long delayed.
Our long dark vigil ends in spring's mild light

And we rise, renewed. Such ritual ignites
The fire in our souls. It's a new day.
In hope, in pain, in song we passed the night.
The long dark vigil ends in spring's mild light.

Land Mass

GETTING TO BLACK EARTH

Start with ocean. A shallow sea, populous
with plankton, and giant fish that feed on it.
Let storms and sunlight flash across the sea.
As bodies die, let them drift down to mud.

Then let there be light. And fire. And heaving:
rock on rock. Let the sea sink. Let it
pour away into other, younger seas.
Let the land rest, damp, exhausted, rich.

Now, let ice appear from north and east
and west. Let it move south to form an isle
of green in a sea of snow. Let this happen over
and over and over for half a million years.

Let low pink quartzite hills hold back the ice.
Let lakes appear beyond, inland seas
with coastlines of blue snow. Let eagles float
above the blue and icy waves, fishing.

Now, catastrophe: Let water break
through ice, drowning bears still sleeping
in their caves, and wolves, and fleeing deer, and mice.
Let a great valley open on the land

marking the pathway of the flood. Let creeks
and rivers deepen crevices in rock,
and gullies form and soften under wind.
Let oaks take root, and shagbark hickory,

and elderberry, yarrow, bee balm, clover,
big and little bluestem, rattlesnake master,
downy gentian, boneset, dogbane, ragweed,
and thickets of sumac, blackberry, blackcap, rose.

Let black soil deepen over limestone seabed
except where it erupts on crowns of hills.
Then, not long ago, let people come.
Start with ocean. End with Black Earth.

EARTHMAKER JUDGES
THE WORLD

Near the top of a Wisconsin hill, a spring erupts
from the point where an underground lake

rests beneath a shale cap and a lower strata
of bedrock dolomite, dense with useful flint.

There sat Earthmaker, Wajaguzera, looking out
over his creation. He could see miles to the north,

to the braided river carved from glacial water,
and south to the region of lead and buffalo; east

to the sacred Four Lakes, which his people marked
with sculptures of migrating bear and deer and birds,

and west, to the great river that drains the continent.
He sat, he saw, he was pleased. At one hand sat

Hinųgaja, his first-born daughter, and on the other,
Wihągaja, the second-born, and among them they judged

that all was good. So they misted the hills with blue smoke,
from which their old name, Xešojera, "smokey mountains."

We call them Blue Mounds now, and few who see their dark
heights know these stories. And without such knowledge,

how do we honor earth, its specific endless beauty? Today,
Blue Mounds means a swimming pool, picnic tables, ski trails.

But Earthmaker's blue tobacco smoke still wreathes the hills,
and his daughters sit beside him, and they see us, and they judge.

CELEBRATION OF THE ORDINARY

"Rule," it means: "the order
of things." From Latin *ordo*,
"a row or rank," from
an even older syllable

meaning "to assemble
skillfully." Ordinary:
sustaining tasks, how we
move through the day,

turning now and again in
comfortable familiarity, in
familiar comfort, to hold
each other's gaze. And

especially: the way of nature,
not just a garden's straight
rows but the winding paths
that deer cut on the prairie,

not only the season's patterns
but a week's changing weather.
"Ordinary" does not mean
predictable, unwavering,

routine, for there is order
seeded into chaos, whose
gorgeous twining patterns
are too huge to discern

from this garden on this day
when we plant ordinary
seeds in ordinary soil,
row upon row upon row,

while across the valley
deer skillfully assemble
networks of pathways
connecting the apple trees.

PLANTING THE VINES

An act of faith:
that thin brown sticks

will soften and bud;
bring forth new leaves;

climb to the trellis
and flower and bear.

To plant, we kneel
in black earth.

BENTWOOD

I thought it would be a willing plant, pliant smooth-barked
tight-budded branches shaped at will to graceful curves.
To build an arbor, I needed willow, so we went
one spring morning to Diana's gone-wild pond.

Diana is herself a gone-wild thing. Maybe she was always
so untrammeled, uncontained. Maybe it came with age.
She's near ninety and as fresh as spring. Her voice is gravel
and her eyes are stars. She's neither bent with age nor broken.

She led us to the bench of sand where willows burst forth
in a tight band of green. In ancient Thrace, Diana's name
would have been Bendis, "bender," goddess of the bonds
of marriage, sculpted holding a small twig to indicate

her control of forces of green growth. In Rome, huntress Diana
was the same, wild herself but controlling all wild urges.
Our Diana is a bit like that. We met her at a fire—not
a wildfire but one of those springtime burns that renew

the land, setting back the buckthorn and honeysuckle,
opening space for burr oak and hickory. She is restoring
oldfields behind her place, inviting back the prairie. Wild
land looks as different from invaded pasture as forest

from cultivated fields, as different as maenads from matrons.
As wildfire is different from these prairie blazes that billow
up on spring nights, ashing the horizon. I remember the first
burned forest I saw, on the Yukon. I was ten. Black trunks

stretched for miles but already fireweed, what Diana calls
the willow-herb, threw a purple carpet on the land. Diana's land
is now ash-black, but by summer flowers will blaze beneath
her cave-filled hills and beside her bubbling spring. Spring:

season of burning, season of bentwood. Falcon and Ruth cut
the willow with us, Falcon wielding her saw like an Amazon
bow, Ruth gathering boughs like a gleaner, bowing and
straightening, bowing and straightening. Soon the truck

is loaded up full. Straight wands, scores of them, tapering
to bendable tips. The breeze quickened as Diana saw us off,
waving promises, "we will be back," as we hauled
the harvest home, divided out our share, and set to work.

We trimmed off branches that went willy-nilly at the nodes,
shooting off at angles where we needed straight and smooth,
then began to measure for our arbor. Up until that moment,
making bentwood from spring willow seemed a way of bending

to the season, a way of tuning ourselves to changing time.
We were bewildered to find the whips so willful. They slipped
from bondage like escaping flames, wanton and wily.
Their curves went hither-thither-yon, wherever they willed.

But we fought the wood, we fought each other. The day grew
chill as we tried to shape three simple curves from wood.
We grew brittle and unbending. The soft spring wood
refused to bend to our design. And so we bent to it.

No good to impose one's will on willow, no good to force
or fetter its native whimsy. Bend with it as it wants to bend.
Follow the lead of the wood. As we learned that, the willow
found its way to arches and arabesques. We bound it

together with tight wires and left it to dry in shape. Then
we poured purple wine and watched the west fill up
with tongues of flame as another field went up in smoke
just as the sun set and a falcon flew across the darkening sky.

THE MEADOW

A chickadee hangs
from one ripe thistle

next to a willow
in the center of

the meadow near
the deep water

And a bee flies
across the umbel

of wild carrot
and the river

breathes slow
tides nearby—

A stone path
winding to the river

And the flowers
swooning over the path

And the river
just about to flood

CONFITEOR: A COUNTRY SONG

Evening. Red sky. Standing at the door
I sense a shadow presence here:
the one who loved this land before.

These harmless hills bear scars of war.
Someone stood here, full of fear.
This is not a metaphor.

Above me, turkey vultures soar;
below the garden, seven deer.
Someone loved this land before,

loved it as I do, maybe more.
She did not simply disappear
and she is not a metaphor:

This was some woman's home before
pale soldiers came to clear
a land that someone loved before.

What to do with facts like this? Ignore
them? Hope they disappear?
Someone loved this land before.
None of this is metaphor.

FORGETTING GOBNAIT

1850: in Tir na Meala, the vale of honey near
Ballyvourney, famine had struck hard, filling

the Macroom workhouse with dying children,
filling Gobnait's cemetery with the dead.

"Much suffering, utter destitution," wrote
Quaker relief workers Wright and Harvey

at the start of the disaster in 1847. But need
was too great. Little was done in Tir na Meala.

The blight passed. Cottages stood empty
where families had died, clutching each other.

1850: in Wisconsin, Black Hawk's people had
been massacred and the land surveyed.

Ebenezer Brigham needed workers. Cheap.
Lead miners, builders, even farmers. Cheap.

They came from Cornwall, where the mines
were dying, they came from Germany where

the risings were suppressed, they came from
Ballyvourney, Gobnait's starving land of honey.

They came from Cork desperate for work, for food.
They came speaking Irish, murmuring together

for they did not speak the language of Earthmaker,
Wajaguzera. They never knew of his nearby

presence at the flint-rich spring on Blue Mounds
nor of his splendid daughters, judging them. Lost

between the loved old land and the stolen new,
they set about forgetting: learned English, built

a church named for an apostle, married Germans.
Around them, bees buzzed through the prairies

and deer wandered among the sessile oaks, Gobnait's
bees, Gobnait's deer, but they set about forgetting her

too, though the land sweeping out from Blue Mounds
looks like Tir na Meala, green and fertile, they set about

forgetting because memory was in their way and they would
never see their home again. They tried to root like prairie

plants, deep into the new soil, but without Gobnait, without
Earthmaker, how does one recognize one's home? They lived,

they thrived, they named the roads Sweeney, Keliher,
Lynch—old Ballyvourney names—and the bees buzzed, and the deer

grazed on the oak mast, and Gobnait joined the daughters
of Earthmaker, watching and judging, waiting to be remembered.

CRANE DANCE

Necks up. Turn. Fan tail. Bow.
Turn again and open wings:

I think of courtly dancers, I think
of mummers, masters of t'ai chi,

ballerinas, shamans; step
and sarabande and promenade,

schottishe and reel and tarantella;
and I decide to join the dance.

I fancy celebrating spring on a greening
field with all these sandhill cranes,

forgetting myself, my human body,
beyond language, beyond thought,

bowing and bending, turning and opening
in warming air, in slanting sun—

but every time I move towards them,
the cranes move off, so that I am

always exactly the same distance
from them. They could fly away

in a rush of wings, abandoning me
to myself, but they do not.

They allow me just this close,
no closer, just this close. And that

becomes their gift to me: later,
days and miles away—and later,

years and continents away—
I can still dance with them from

this distance that makes me human,
still hear them speak in that distinct

vocabulary of longing and grace,
connection and presence; their gift to me.

THE YEAR IN APPLES

January

Snow outlines the limbs
of a small tree on the hill:
Snow Apple, famous for
bleached-white flesh stained
red beneath its skin.

Snow covers the woodpile.
I brush it off and bring
apple wood inside,
best for winter heat,
better even than oak.

February

My friend grew old
this winter. I had not
noticed until tonight
at dinner, when I saw
how her skin no longer
fit her face, how flesh
had thinned behind
her still-red cheeks.

March

Mid-day: the deer
paw at corn stubble
in the fields,
so hungry they leave
forest edges and
shadows of dusk.

We toss the last few
apples and turnips,
withered and pale,
in a heap near the barn.
The next morning,
streams of footprints.

April

With an herb
omelet, first
harvest of spring

we eat applesauce,
the last of last
fall's bounty.

May

We have three cider
trees, old seedling apples,
down beside the road.

They bear heavily,
small tart fruit
of unknown species.

Apple cores, tossed aside
a century ago, have become
these blossoming towers.

June

In the month of no apples,
our friends buy an orchard.

We walk under the trees,
their heavy blooms promising

pies and sauce and relish.
We promise we'll bring

our cider press over, come fall.
Then we eat raspberries and cream.

July

The apples are not ripe,
I tell them, but my friend

holds his granddaughter
up to the tree and she,

laughing, grabs a small
green apple and bites

into it. Everything is
shining, shining.

August

From scarcity to surplus:
this week we picked
two bushels of yellow apples
from a tree that has never
fruited since we moved here.

The girl who grew up playing
under empty branches climbs
into the tree's heart and picks
with both hands. She drops
apples on us, a rain of gold.

September

Perfect apples are falling
from the trees, landing hard
but unbruised on seeding grass.

All weekend we pressed cider,
sweated apples with
loose skins, hard green apples

we had to cut before grinding,
small apples and large,
unblemished apples and apples

kissed by worms and flies.
Apples rain down, so many
that we throw them to the cows,

overwhelmed by exuberance
and plenty. Fruit litters the ground
like blossoms in spring.

October

Neighbors up the road carry apples,
cut in quarters, in big ice-chests.

They are eighty and strong, but
bring grandsons to do the work.

One turns the grinder, the other
rotates the screw atop the press.

Cider pours out, dark and rich.
We drink, each of us, from cups

held by another. There is nothing
like it: this first taste of fall.

November

Sometime in blurred summer
I put up this pie—savory
and spicy, packed with sugared
apples, frozen now for months.
I do not remember the day
I picked the apples, made the pie.
Will I remember today?

December

We put apples, wrapped in paper,
in the cellar, too near the onions
and potatoes that begin to
soften as though spring's sweet
breath warmed them into growth.
We move the apples to the porch,
and everything slips back to sleep.

Every apple I unwrap is twig
and blossom, branch and leaf,
blossom spring and cider fall,
the fragrance and the taste
of growth and death and time.
I breathe it in, all of it, and bite.

LESSON OF THE BEES

The steady traffic in that corner
of the garden is so obvious now,

especially when evening's slant light
gilds the travelers swooping down

to that flat rock I now know rests
beneath the lilies and white phlox,

that gateway to the city of bees
with its rooms of secret paper

where the news is all of flowers
and the appetites of queens.

How many years of bee time
have passed since last week

when, blindly weeding, I came
too close to those city gates?

So fast. So fast. I did not think
"bee" or "sting" or "run," so fast

did she strike, so fast did I run.
In beeland's history of struggle

surely that battle is remembered.
And what of the small warrior

who gave her life to drive me off?
Heroic ballads in bee measure

are surely sung to her when bards
relate the history of the tribe.

Do they mention, I wonder, that
her venom now runs in my blood?

THINGS TO BELIEVE IN

trees, in general; oaks, especially;
burr oaks that survive fire, in particular;
and the generosity of apples

seeds, all of them: carrots like dust,
winged maple, doubled beet, peach kernel;
the inevitability of change

frogsong in spring; cattle
lowing on the farm across the hill;
the melodies of sad old songs

comfort of savory soup;
sweet iced fruit; the aroma of yeast;
a friend's voice; hard work

seasons; bedrock; lilacs;
moonshadows under the ash grove;
something breaking through

YOUNG DEER

At the sharp bend in the forest path
where I had seen her with her mother

she was there, all gangly adolescence
and liquid eyes and high white tail,

but alone, it being the time of year
when deer send forth their young

and start the cycle over: a gray shadow
of solitude barely visible in the trees,

she stared at me. I stared back at her.
The moment was as still as death.

Then I put my hands atop my head
to mimic ears, and waved at her.

She started. I thought she would run.
And she did. But not away—towards me—

I think now I saw a hungry urgency
about her eyes, a startled longing, or

perhaps I just imagined that I recognized
a common yearning. She stopped short

a few yards from me, looked at me
sidewides, one great dark eye filling

with recognition. A shudder. Then
she was gone, tail white in the brush.

But then she turned again and stared.
And stood quite still, as I did, and then

took a dozen dainty steps towards me
until she stood, breathing hard, not

ten feet away. If I thought I understood
what had brought her near before—

an orphan's sharp wild hope—everything
was alien this time, I have no idea why

she chose to come back and stand staring
at me once she knew I was a stranger.

It was something about love, I think.
Something about walking through fear.

TRANSUBSTANTIATION

Sunday. End of summer.
Cloudless sky. A flight of geese.

And the day's epistle reads,
"I bud forth delights like the vine,

my blossoms become fruit
fair and rich, I am the mother

of fair love and of fear and
of knowledge and of holy hope,

come to me, be filled with fruit,"
for it is the vigil of the virgin

ascending, the day we climb to
the bishop's vineyard. Just weeks

to harvest, grapes rich and fair.
The sumac flames, the geese cry out,

the asters bloom, the apples fall.
From soil and stone, the vines ascend.

WILDNESS AND GRACE

Wild grapes tangle with wild plums
just where the road turns west.
When clouds of blossoms floated there
last spring, we felt blessed

by promises of summer fruit.
We didn't see the vines
twisting up the slender trees
until today. To find

the dust-blue grapes ripe among
the sunset plums was grace
itself: "grace," from *gratus*,
pleasing, grateful; the embrace

of splendid momentary life,
the unsought present.
We fill our hands and baskets
with wild, luxuriant,

unexpected gifts. Come cold,
come snow, come winter's night,
we will have summer once again:
plum wine in firelight

and purple jelly on warm bread.
Snow and blossom, past
and future, world and spirit, all
in this moment: fleeting, vast.

THE LATE GARDEN

1

Before ripeness
an intenser green.

2

Sharp blood-smell
where the dog has
crushed a leaf.
Overhead, sudden
winds rake the trees.

3

I lose my ring while
harvesting late tomatoes.
I bend to search.
So many golds!
Loss opening my eyes—

4

The story of a tomato
is the story of any
other tomato.
The story of a life
is the story of any
other life.

5

As I cannot tell
you any other
way, let me
try this:
I yearn to let you
eat a ripe tomato
from my hand,
with no salt.

6

The vine dreams tomatoes.
The tomatoes dream the vine.

7

I have emptied
the garden
at last. Frost
burned my hands.
When I lifted them
to my cheeks, I
was stung red.
I left behind
nothing, nothing.

STORM LESSONS

1. Somewhere, right now, one is brewing.

2. The wind is not trying to get in.

3. In high winds, songbirds sing.

4. It is not storms that rage and batter.

5. Butterflies migrate within.

6. The beauty of inky clouds
   over a churning white lake and
   the beauty of a still summer meadow
   are equivalent.

7. Storms storm. It's nothing personal.

8. They end.

HARVEST EVENING

Across the valley, prairie grasses blaze
pink and scarlet in the dying sun.
Beside the bronze of brittle corn, just days
past harvest, the goldenrod is stiff and brown.

A few flowers cling: boneset, aster,
chrysanthemum, a final floral clock.
Everywhere, the death, the seeds. Burrs
bristle on the tall stems of the dock.

Rowan and crabapple and viburnum
echo the bloody color in the west,
while above it all the hawk's wings drum
assuring that no small thing finds its nest.

TURN, TURN, TURN

The little
rag-eared doe

does not run
when I approach

because I have
for months

imitated her
when we meet:

head cocked,
hands atop head

waving like ears,
foot pawing ground,

but today,
for no reason—

unless because
spring is near—

I wanted to be
human to her

and spoke low
words, aimless

sounds crossing
the frozen stream

between us,
and she did not

run but stared
and then, for no

reason—unless
wordless yearning

is a reason—I began
to sing, the one song

that came to my mind:
to everything

there is a season
and a time

for every purpose
under heaven:

a time to be born,
I sang to the deer,

a time to die,
and she moved closer,

a time to rend,
a time to sew,

a time we may embrace
—a deep sudden

groaning silenced me
as the deer froze, liquid

eyes locked with mine,
and between us

the ice cracked apart

MAN'DO IS GOOD, I SLEPT

From the diaries of Fidelia Fielding,
last speaker of Mohegan, 1902-04

December

I watch the dawn come, then warm noon,
soon it is night, so soon the sun goes.

I saw a fox this morning, and a hound
following it, then snow fell into night.

January

The sun rises, then it is noon,
already noon, then already night.

I live to see another dawn. It is cold.
Snow is falling. Soon noon, soon night.

April

Windy. Wind goes by, whistling.
The sun is good, rising in clear sky.

Thank you for food, great earth.
I do not fear anything now.

May

Drizzling rain. People say too much,
half of what they say is untrue.

Man'do is good and strengthens me.
I am strong enough to care for myself.

Sun rising early, I find eggs so that
I do not die of hunger, it is very cold.

June

Clouds, rain, cold. I saw a snake:
fish in its mouth, could not bite me.

Poor white people. They want money. But
they cannot carry it away when they die,

The sun rises, then it clouds over.
Man'do is good, all things are good.

WAYS TO LEAVE

From the hilltop, take the old road
west and steeply downhill towards
Blue Mounds where Earthmaker sits
to judge the world.

Or trace the creek. It rises near
the hilltop and meanders southwards
to the river. Or go straight
over the crest

and southeast down to Black Earth Creek
where herons fish and deer graze
beside the fields. So many ways
to leave

this place or anyplace. And so few
ways to stay: as limestone from
an ancient sea; as shadow, bone
and dust.

Acknowledgements

Many of the poems in the second section, "Land Mass," were published in the chapbook *Grace of Ancient Land* from the *Voices from the American Land* program.

The following poems have appeared in journals:

"Confiteor: A Country Song in *The Aldo Leopold Outlook*, 2012.

"Ways to Leave" in *Verse Wisconsin*, 2010.

"Lessons from Birds" (as "The Bird Oracles") in *Issues in Study of Literature and Environment* (ISLE), 2009.

"Wildness and Grace, "Transubstantiation," and "Planning the Vineyard" in *Alimentum: The Journal of Food*, 2006.

"Storm Lessons" in *Issues in Study of Literature and Environment* (ISLE), 2003.

"Crane Dance" in *Whole Terrain*, 2005.

The following poems have appeared in anthologies:

"Celebrating the Ordinary." In *The Poet's Quest for God*. Todd Swift, ed., 2012

"Confetior: A Country Song." In *Villanelles*, Annie Finch and Marie-Elizabeth Mali, eds., 2012.

"Connemara Autumn." In *Ecopoetry: A Contemporary American Anthology*, Ann Fisher-Wirth, editor, 2012.

"Storm Lessons." In *Brute Neighbors: Urban Nature Poetry, Prose and Photography*, Chris Green and Liam Heneghan, eds, 2011.

"Young Deer," in *What's Nature Got to Do with Me?: Staying Wildly Sane in a Mad World*, Yvette Schnoeker-Shorb, ed., 2010.

"Keeping Vigil in Renvyle" (as "A House in Renvyle") in *Salmon: A Journey in Poetry*, 2007.

"Wind Liturgy" (as "What the Wind Said") in *Irish-American Poetry*. Dan Tobin, editor. Notre Dame University Press, 2005.

Photograph © Linda Schwartz Photograher, Chicago Il

PATRICIA MONAGHAN was Professor of Interdisciplinary Studies at De Paul University, Chicago. Her several Irish related works include, *Irish Spirit: Pagan, Celtic, Christian, Global*, an international collection of essays which she compiled and edited for Wolfhound Press in 2001. Her poetry collection *Dancing with Chaos* (SalmonPoetry, 2002) notably delights in the entanglements of the human and personal in poetry and science. Patricia was honored with a Pushcart Prize, the Paul Gruchow Nature Writing award, and the Friends of Literature award for poetry. She and her husband, Michael McDermott, founded The Black Earth Institute, a writers & artists think-tank whose current Fellows come from all over North America and Ireland, and she was vice-President of the Association for the Study of Women and Mythology as well as a lecturer for the Women's theological Institute. Patricia died on 11 November 2012.